www.providencebooks.net

Publisher Contact

Email:contact@providencebooks.net

Social media: facebook.com/providencebooks

Acknowledgements

The team at Providence Books would like to thank our friends, family, suppliers and customers for making our vision of creating the highest-quality books a reality. Thanks for purchasing and enjoy the quotes!

This page is intentionally left blank

This page is intentionally left blank

A lot of directors in my experience are very receptive. They see what you do first, and then they want to find a place to put the camera, and they tweak you here and there.

Annette Bening

Acting is not about being famous, it's about exploring the human soul.

Annette Bening

And if there's anything movies can do in a way that I just love, and I love as an audience is, 'Show me something I don't know about. Show me something I haven't seen.'

Annette Bening

Anybody who has children and children who are well feels a sense of responsibility towards parents and kids and families that are struggling and that aren't well.

Annette Bening

Anyone who is drawn in broad strokes either negatively or positively is generally not very interesting to play.

Annette Bening

By the time I was in high school, Roe v. Wade had passed, so that was also happening; girls were getting pregnant and getting abortions - and that happened in my school too.

Annette Bening

Critics have a responsibility to put things in a cultural and sociological or political context. That is important.

Annette Bening

Even with a stable character, you want something surprising to happen, hopefully because that's what the camera loves the most. That's what is great about film.

Annette Bening

Every person's opinion, in a way, does matter.

Annette Bening

Everybody has a public life, and they have their own private life. Everybody has their secrets. Everybody has their own private, you know, agonies as well as joys. And that's what great drama, whether it's the movies or the theater, that's what it shows.

Annette Bening

Five billion people have played Hamlet. 'To be or not to be.'
And how do you do that and find your way into your own
journey, your own way of telling it?

Annette Bening

Getting all dressed up and putting on fancy clothes - all of
that's a great thing, but oddly, it doesn't really have a lot to do
with acting most of the time.

Annette Bening

Glamour is really fun.

Annette Bening

Having a life outside of movies is like pure oxygen. It makes
the work more precious and informed.

Annette Bening

I always wonder about people's history and their lives,
especially people that are a little bit more distant, who
obviously have had some kind of a thing, and you know there's
some reason why they're not able to connect. It's not because
they don't want to. They don't have the ability.

Annette Bening

I am in awe of Ruth Draper.

Annette Bening

I am really looking forward as I get older and older, to being less and less nice.

Annette Bening

I didn't do a movie until I was almost 30. I'm grateful for that because it gave me a chance to be an adult in the world and do work in the regional theater that very few people cared about. I loved it and I wanted to do that stuff.

Annette Bening

I didn't picture myself as a movie actress. I began to think about it around college. I remember thinking, 'Well somebody has to be in them,' so maybe I could do that eventually. It's all been a surprise.

Annette Bening

I do have to take care of myself, not only because I'm in the movies, just for mental health reasons. I exercise for me. You know, maybe it would be nice to not have to do that in order to feel good, but I do. I feel like I have to, to feel good. To clear my head and all of that, so.

Annette Bening

I don't really have a choice. I'm getting older.

Annette Bening

I don't see myself as competing with other actresses. I mean, I went through a time when I was in New York, and I was going to lots of auditions and trying to get parts, but even then, you're not really competing with the other actresses. There is a competition going on, but it's not like something you can win in that way.

Annette Bening

I don't see myself as having to compete with younger actresses; I don't feel that.

Annette Bening

I feel really lucky that I'm able to pursue the work that I love. I want my children to see that. I want them to have that for themselves, something that they love, that they do, that they pursue in their lives as a way of growing and learning.

Annette Bening

I feel that certain things are best kept inside a family and not discussed with anyone else.

Annette Bening

I feel very lucky I don't have to be a critic.

Annette Bening

I feel very, very lucky to have come from the family I did. We have our dysfunctions and our problems, just like any family. But my parents are extremely loving people.

Annette Bening

I find the reality of our emotional lives interesting.

Annette Bening

I had never been attracted to younger guys. I had, from my late teens, always liked men who were older than me.

Annette Bening

I have huge chunks of time when I'm not working.

Annette Bening

I have perfected the art of putting my feet on my husband's lap during awards ceremonies so he can rub them.

Annette Bening

I just want to be educated.

Annette Bening

I knew I wanted children in my life. The acting was always in
relation to it. Life at home is chaos. They're wonderful. They're
such interesting human beings. I just love it. I'm lucky.

Annette Bening

I like that I've been through things, that when something
happens, it resonates with something that already happened.
It's not that things like loss are more or less painful. But they're
deeper. I find that fascinating.

Annette Bening

I like things that I feel comfortable in.

Annette Bening

I love being busy, and I love having a lot going on; it's
exciting.

Annette Bening

I love the craft of acting, I love learning, I love everything that comes with the new project; the whole process is totally intoxicating to me.

Annette Bening

I love the luxury of the camera. The camera does so much for you. I like the secrets a camera can tell.

Annette Bening

I never speak for my husband, and I never speak for my children. It's a rule. Believe me, it is.

Annette Bening

I never thought my private life would be newsworthy.

Annette Bening

I read 'Game Change.' If you want to relive the campaign, that book is unbelievable. It's great. It's the book of that campaign. It brought all the memories back of everything with Clinton and Obama, and Sarah Palin and McCain, and choosing her, and John Edwards. It was an interesting book.

Annette Bening

I remember hearing someone say that good acting is more about taking off a mask than putting one on, and in movie acting, certainly that's true. With the camera so close, you can see right down into your soul, hopefully. So being able to do that in a way is terrifying, and in another way, truly liberating. And I like that about it.

Annette Bening

I saw a Shakespeare play when I was - I guess I was in junior high. And I just fell in love with the theater because, for me, it was a combination of big ideas and feeling.

Annette Bening

I still remember the five points of salesmanship: attention, interest, conviction, desire and close.

Annette Bening

I think for all of us, as we age, there are always a few moments when you are shocked.

Annette Bening

I think in the past, around the time that method acting became so prevalent, it used to be that American actors were thought to be the kind that would work more from the inside out, and that the English actors worked more from the outside in.

Annette Bening

I think people have a right to their point of view.

Annette Bening

I think we as celebrities have a lot more control.

Annette Bening

I think what's interesting about the whole paparazzi thing is that unless you're Brad Pitt or Madonna, you can pretty much avoid it. You know when you're going to an opening that you will be photographed, so that's fine. And you know the restaurants that have paparazzi, so you don't go to them.

Annette Bening

I think when you're at your best as an actor, it is cathartic.

Annette Bening

I think you sort of shed skins as you go along in life. You get into your 40s, and you feel like, 'OK, no more pretending.' You get to just be who you are.

Annette Bening

I wanted to be a classical actress. I plodded along. I went to junior college in San Francisco, I was in a Repertory Company. My hero was Eva Le Gallienne, who was a great theater actress at the turn of the century who created her own company, and she wrote these hilarious autobiographies at the time.

Annette Bening

I'm certainly not a perfect mother, but I am an avid mother, let me put it that way.

Annette Bening

I'm interested in writing that explores all sides of human beings.

Annette Bening

I'm lucky: almost all my family has lived to be very old. I have one grandfather who lived to be 100.

Annette Bening

I'm still very critical of myself in film.

Annette Bening

I've always been pretty levelheaded. In show business, you need to have a certain internal stability.

Annette Bening

I've made some movies that I really loved that nobody saw.

Annette Bening

I've played parts that were just likable people, and there's a certain pleasure in that. And that's that.

Annette Bening

I've tried to take roles with great demands.

Annette Bening

If anything, I want to please people too much.

Annette Bening

If you can open people's hearts first, then maybe people's minds get opened after that.

Annette Bening

It used to be the one or the other, right? You were the 'bad girl' or the 'good girl' or the 'bad mother' or 'the good mother,' 'the horrible businesswoman who eschewed her children' or 'the earth mother who was happy to be at home baking pies,' all of that stuff that we sort of knew was a lie.

Annette Bening

It's always 'busy' with four children; it's chaos.

Annette Bening

It's easier to see in someone else, another actor, how they kind of disappear and then this other persona appears. A great actor is a thing of mystery.

Annette Bening

It's hard to make a living in this business. Unions aren't as strong as they used to be. For a journeyman actor - someone who doesn't have a famous name but has consistent work in theater or film or TV - it has become harder to get through, harder to raise a family.

Annette Bening

It's kind of a mystery to me, as far as my own life experiences and what I've witnessed - why some people can just move on through traumatic experiences, in childhood particularly, and why other people are just paralyzed by it. I just don't know how and why that is.

Annette Bening

Most people are looking for something to give their life meaning.

Annette Bening

Most women would say they relate to 'Hedda Gabler' - there's a part of her in them. Ibsen was writing about a deep ambivalence that many women feel about domesticity. I think about myself and friends of mine - we have some of Hedda's qualities and traits.

Annette Bening

My character in 'Running With Scissors' is manic-depressive. She starts out as a wonderfully eccentric person, and then descends into a terrible illness.

Annette Bening

My dad was in the life insurance business, so I learned about selling when I was about 14 because I started working as a secretary.

Annette Bening

My husband and I have very similar backgrounds even though we're years apart. So there are a lot of things that we basically share.

Annette Bening

My mother is not somebody who's troubled by aging.

Annette Bening

My parents were very supportive. They went to every show. And they never told me not to do what I was doing.

Annette Bening

My sister and I fought a lot when we were kids. I was the little bratty sister, and she would kind of walk away, not wanting to be associated with me.

Annette Bening

Oh, honey, I'm from Oklahoma! This is who I am - middle-class all the way!

Annette Bening

Our children see us a certain way, and we want to be seen by them in a certain way. I certainly want to be a strong, stable, loving, consistent presence in my children's lives. But we are human beings, too.

Annette Bening

Right now, I love the fact that I have so many opportunities, but I know this privileged position cannot last. That doesn't mean that I'll stop working. I picture myself as an old actress doing cameos in films with people saying: 'Isn't that that Bening woman?'

Annette Bening

Somebody said something really smart: It's like you end up being the defense attorney for your role. Your job is to defend their point of view. You're fighting for what they want. You learn that in acting school - it's Acting 1A: 'What do you want? What's in the way?'

Annette Bening

Sometimes you're reading something, and you don't know it will be important in your life. You're reading this script, and you start to get involved. It's not an intellectual experience.

Annette Bening

The tension I feel is the moment they say, 'Action!' Movies are like lightning in a bottle, and you always want to find when you possibly can catch a surprising moment.

Annette Bening

The time I spend with my kids informs every fiber of who I am.

Annette Bening

There are so many different kinds of relationships, so it's sort of difficult to define what is considered normal.

Annette Bening

There's love for your parents, your family, your spouse, your partner, your friends, but the nature of the connection you have with your child, there's nothing like it. It has its own character and it's so serious and so powerful, and so it's a prism through which I see everything.

Annette Bening

There's no question that you can explore aspects of yourself through roles that you play, and you get a chance to investigate yourself; that's healthy, and it's therapeutic in a way. But if you're indulging yourself, exploration at the cost of the story or the project, that's not good.

Annette Bening

There's so much of our psychological makeup which is impermissible for us to explore because it's inappropriate or perverse or scary. I'm interested in exploring that in myself. I try to be honest with myself about everything that I feel. I'm not saying I'm able to do that all the time, but it's something I'm interested in.

Annette Bening

To me idealized characters are so boring to play, especially having grown up in the classical theater. That's a great experience, but as a woman, especially, you've played a lot of idealized characters. So when you've got someone who has weaknesses as well as strengths, that's interesting.

Annette Bening

We all get lost along the way, but hopefully we figure out some sort of path. It helps if you can imagine the process as well as the goal. Those kinds of dreams are easier to achieve.

Annette Bening

We all perform our lives in a way. And the actor is a perfect metaphor to get at that theme of 'how do we find our authentic selves?' And that we all - whether we're actors or not - perform ourselves. As a way of searching. As a way of fumbling around and trying to say, is this my voice? Is this who I am?

Annette Bening

We still want to idealize moms, and sometimes we want to idealize actresses who are moms, too. I know that's something I've experienced, but we're all just doing the best we can and we're all trying to raise our kids and talk to them about everything that needs to be discussed.

Annette Bening

What makes us love a character is a character that tries.

Annette Bening

What really motivates you to try to work things out as an actor is in large part fear, because you want to get into that narrative and bring the audience along.

Annette Bening

When I look at women, older than I am, in their 50s, 60, 70s, 80s, and I see women that I admire, I think, 'Oh, I get it; that's how I'm going to be.' I'm not scared. I want to be that.

Annette Bening

When I started in the theater, I'd do plays by Shakespeare or Ibsen or Chekhov, and they all created great women's roles.

Annette Bening

When I started, I was a theater actress, and there were roles that I couldn't imagine not playing, like Rosalind in 'As You Like It.' I used to think I would die if I could play that. But then I started doing movies, and I had children, and I moved to Los Angeles. And now I kind of can't remember what those roles would be.

Annette Bening

When I watch my kids, and I see the primal level at which the sibling relationships are formed, then I completely understand what these unresolved adult sibling problems are based on. You know, 'Mom liked you better' and, 'You got your own room and I didn't.'

Annette Bening

With movies, so much of it is, 'Who is the human being that is going to be directing it?' Because it is their medium. In a way, you are serving the director, and when it is someone that you feel you can have a lot of confidence in, it can make a big difference.

Annette Bening

Yes, I know I've played these women, but I'm not really conniving at all.

Annette Bening

This page is intentionally left blank

This page is intentionally left blank

This page is intentionally left blank

This page is intentionally left blank

This page is intentionally left blank

www.ingramcontent.com/pod-product-compliance
Lightning Source LLC
Chambersburg PA
CBHW072021290526
45787CB00013B/1695